Bear Buddies
A Child Learns to Make Friends

"A friend loves at all times."

Proverbs 17:17

We all want friends. However, having friends is not always as easy as it looks. Before we can *have* a friend, we must learn to *be* a friend. *Bear Buddies* will help you teach your children some of the simple, but important, skills that are necessary for being a friend and for making and keeping friends.

A BEAR HUGS BOOK ™

Love Bears All Things: A Child Learns to Love

Bear Up: A Child Learns to Handle Ups and Downs

Bearing Burdens: A Child Learns to Help

Bear Buddies: A Child Learns to Make Friends

Bearing Fruit: A Child Learns About the Fruit of the Spirit

I Can Bearly Wait: A Child Learns Patience

Titles in Preparation:

Bears Repeating: A Child Learns Thankfulness

You are Beary Special: A Child Learns Self-esteem

Bear Necessities: A Child Learns Obedience

Bear Facts: A Child Learns Truthfulness

Bearing Good News: A Child Learns to Be Positive

Sweeter Than Honey: A Child Learns the Golden Rule

Copyright 1986, Paul C. Brownlow
Hardcover, ISBN: 0-915720-55-8
Library Edition, ISBN: 0-915720-56-6

Brownlow Publishing Company, Inc.
6309 Airport Freeway, Fort Worth, Texas 76117

Bear Buddies
A Child Learns to Make Friends

By

Pat Kirk & Alice Brown

Illustrated by

Diann Bartnick

BROWNLOW PUBLISHING COMPANY, INC.

Without a friend, life would be just

like sitting on an old hollow log.

But as soon as a friend comes along

...presto! We play leapfrog.

But how can I make a friend?
Do I just get on a log
and wait for magic to begin?

Maybe the wind will blow one in?
No, my friend, watch me.
I'll show you how to begin.

Don't sit around and sulk or stew,
ask a friend to play with you.

Just walk up with a happy grin
and say, "Let's play. I'll be your friend."

Don't get attention with a kick or a slap.

Your friend might feel hurt and kick you back.

Then your friendship

will be on the wrong track.

Instead, play the friendship game.

Start by learning your friends' names.

Then they'll want to learn your name.

That's the way to win the friendship game.

Be choosy as you pick your friends.

Try to choose other good citizens.

A friend who always gets into trouble

will take you with him—double trouble!

Show your friends you really care.

Don't just stand there and stare.

Look at your friends right in the eyes.

They'll listen to you. What a surprise!

Don't always tell your friends what to do.

They will soon get tired of you!

Try, instead, to ask politely.

Then most friends will say, "Yes" most likely.

When your guests come to play,

let them pick the games that day.

Then when it's time to visit them,

You will be a welcome friend.

Try to imagine how others feel
and why they act as they do.

You'll grow to know your friend better,

and learn more about yourself, too!

And when it's time to eat a snack,
serve your guest first. You stand back.

Let your friend be first to choose,

when you're serving cake for two.

But if a friend just won't play,

unless you let him have his way,

then tell him he can go on home.

He'll soon learn it's no fun alone.

Be even more careful with your friend's
toys than you are with your own.

People and bears who tear up things,

will end up all alone.

Yes, friendship is more than
strolling arm in arm,
or learning to use charm.

It's more than knowing what to say
while having fun
on a sunny day.

Friendship is caring and sharing,
   taking turns and having fun.

Friends help friends,
   no matter what comes.

Take care of yourself and others
   your whole life long.

And God will help
   to keep your friendships strong.

CHRISTIAN LEARNING CENTER
MINISTRY OF SILVERTON FRIENDS CHURCH